Bridging the Gender Pay Gap in Law Firms

Author
Stephanie Hawthorne

Managing director
Sian O'Neill

Bridging the Gender Pay Gap in Law Firms
is published by

Globe Law and Business Ltd
3 Mylor Close
Horsell
Woking
Surrey GU21 4DD
United Kingdom
Tel: +44 20 3745 4770
www.globelawandbusiness.com

Printed and bound by CPI Group (UK) Ltd, Croydon CR0 4YY, United Kingdom

Bridging the Gender Pay Gap in Law Firms

ISBN 9781787422124
EPUB ISBN 9781787422131
Adobe PDF ISBN 9781787422148
Mobi ISBN 9781787422155

Table of contents

Introduction

Excessive executive pay and the gender pay gap are at root an issue of fairness. It is unacceptable that in 2018, men and women are rewarded so differently for doing the same jobs.

"Transparency on gender pay gaps must only be the beginning. We want to examine the actions necessary to close the gender pay gap and ensure women have a genuine opportunity to get the top jobs."[1]

These are the telling words of Member of Parliament Rachel Reeves, chair of the Business, Energy and Industrial Strategy (BEIS) Committee, which recently examined the gender pay gap in the United Kingdom.

In law firms, as in much of the rest of British industry, the gender pay gap is considerable. Much more needs to be done to achieve equality, although the profession has come a long way since Carrie Morison became the country's first female solicitor. This followed the Sex Disqualification (Removal) Act 1919, which paved the way for the first women lawyers.[2]

At the time of her entry to the profession, Morison claimed, in an interview published in the *Dundee Evening Telegraph* on 31 October 1922: "Men say the law is too rough and tumble for women."[3] She and thousands of her successors have since proved them wrong: today there are now more female than male solicitors[4] and women made up 61.6% of new admissions in 2016/17.

The Law Society of England and Wales' annual statistics report for 2017[5] shows that there are 139,624 solicitors with practising certificates – a 2.5% increase on 2016 figures and broadly in line with annual growth over the last 10 years. Women now make up 50.1% of the 139,624 practising certificate holders; but figures from the Solicitors Regulation Authority show that in 2017, women made up 59% of non-partner solicitors, compared to just 33% of partners (up from 31% in 2014).[6] The difference is greater still in the largest firms (50-plus partners), where just 29% of partners are female.

There have still been small but welcome signs of progress in the largest firms, however, as the gap has narrowed over the past four years, with the proportion of female partners rising steadily from 25% in 2014 to 29% in 2017.

Women solicitors are younger on average (40 years) than male solicitors (45 years).

Commenting on the figures, Law Society President Joe Egan said: "With more women than men and a steadily growing proportion of solicitors from a black, Asian and minority ethnic background, it is more important than ever the profession recognises and rewards talent equally. An important foundation is transparency, and this includes gender pay gap reporting."

Gender pay gap reporting – the law

The Equality Act 2010 (Gender Pay Gap Information) Regulations 2017 oblige employers with 250 or more employees to publish information relating to the gender pay gap in their organisations. In particular, employers are required to publish:

- the difference between the average hourly rate of pay paid to male and female employees;
- the difference between the average bonus paid to male and female employees;
- the proportions of male and of female employees who receive bonuses; and
- the relative proportions of male and female employees in each quartile pay band of the workforce.

For the purposes of these regulations, 'employment' is defined in Section 83 of the Equality Act 2010 and includes employment under a contract of employment, a contract of apprenticeship or a contract personally to do work.[7]

Law firm Lewis Silkin has produced a helpful internal note[8] which explains the law on gender pay gap reporting and has kindly allowed extracts to be reproduced here:

"Transparency on gender pay gaps must only be the beginning. We want to examine the actions necessary to close the gender pay gap and ensure women have a genuine opportunity to get the top jobs."

Rachel Reeves MP

- *Employers in the UK with 250 or more "relevant employees" must report 6 pieces of information.*
  - *Mean/median pay gaps*
  - *Mean/median bonus gaps*
  - *Headcount by quartile (M%/F%)*
  - *Proportion of men/women receiving a bonus*
- *"Relevant employees" is broadly defined and included self-employed contractors (although they are some exemptions that might apply when it is unreasonably difficult to collect pay data on these individuals).*
- *The pay gaps are based on what each relevant employee is paid on 5 April each year. Hourly rates are calculated from what people are paid, then the mean and median hourly rates for men and women are compared.*
- *Bonus gaps are for the 12 months previous to 5 April. The mean and median man and woman are similarly compared (although only those that received a bonus are counted – meaning that a company that pays small bonuses to female dominated roles such as secretaries can improve their bonus gaps by instead just paying no bonuses at all).*

The Gender Pay Gap Regulations cover primarily UK workers, but employees based overseas must be included if they have an employment contract that is subject to the law of England and Wales or Scotland.[9]

Spotlight on gender pay gap data

1. Results

The United Kingdom is one of the few countries in the world to require employers to publish such comprehensive gender pay gap data. For the first time ever, 100% of UK employers identified as falling within the scope of the gender pay gap regulations have published their data: all 10,000 UK employers identified by the government as having over 250 workers have now published this data.[10]

The data shows that:

- more than three out of four in-scope UK companies pay their male staff more on average than their female staff;
- more than half give higher bonuses to men on average than women; and
- more than 80% have more women in their lowest-paid positions than in their highest-paid positions.

Commenting on the figures, Minister for Women and Equalities Penny Mordaunt said: "It is appalling that in the 21st century there is still a big difference between the average earnings of men and women. While I am encouraged that over 10,000 employers have published their data, these figures set out in real terms for the first time some of the challenges and the scale of this issue."

Equality and Human Rights Commission Chief Executive Rebecca Hilsenrath said:

> *Building on the work by the Government Equalities Office, our enforcement approach has proved to be successful, resulting in full compliance by all those considered to be in scope.*
>
> *We have been clear that it is not only the right thing to do but that we would use all our enforcement powers where employers failed to report. They have taken our warnings seriously and avoided costly court action. We will now be turning our attention to the accuracy of reporting.*

The first gender pay gap reports were all filed by 5 April 2018. People were scandalised by the huge inequality in remuneration levels across all sectors of British industry. The bold statistics by themselves reveal little, other than a shameful gap between the respective earnings of women and men. Tables 1 to 5 show the gender pay gap and bonus gap in the top 50 UK law firms (in order of 2017 revenue). Table 6 shows the gender pay gap and bonus gap in the Magic Circle firms, and Table 7 shows the gender pay gap and bonus gap in US and international firms based in the United Kingdom.

Table 1. Top 50 law firms – gender pay gap (hourly rate)

No	Firm	Mean gender pay gap %	Median gender pay gap %
1	Addleshaw Goddard*	23.8%	16.4%
2	Allen & Overy	19.8%	27.4%
3	Ashurst	24.8%	32.7%
4	Berwin Leighton Paisner	22.3%	36.8%
5	Bird & Bird	14.5%	27.6%
6	Blake Morgan	26.1%	32.8%
7	BLM	18.4%	22.4%
8	Burges Salmon	23.3%	35.2%
9	Charles Russell Speechlys	22.0%	28.1%
10	Clifford Chance	20.3%	37.2%
11	Clyde & Co	22.4%	38.2%
12	CMS	17.3%	32.8%
13	DAC Beachcroft	27.1%	22.6%
14	DLA Piper	17.8%	12.2%
15	DWF	23.7%	26.5%
16	Eversheds Sunderland	23.2%	25.4%
17	Fieldfisher	16.5%	22.2%
18	Freeths*	11.0%	8.8%
19	Freshfields Bruckhaus Deringer	13.9%	13.3%
20	Gateley (a)	47.7%	51.6%

21	Gowling WLG*	25.0%	25.0%
22	Herbert Smith Freehills*	19.0%	38.8%
23	Hill Dickinson	25.9%	23.5%
24	Hogan Lovells	15.3%	26.0%
25	Holman Fenwick Willan	17.4%	30.9%
26	Ince & Co	28.0%	42.0%
27	Irwin Mitchell	12.8%	15.9%
28	Kennedys	22.2%	25.9%
29	Linklaters	23.2%	39.1%
30	Macfarlanes	16.5%	37.1%
31	Mills & Reeve	20.1%	34.2%
32	Mishcon de Reya	17.3%	37.4%
33	Norton Rose Fulbright	17.0%	23.8%
34	Osborne Clarke	24.4%	31.7%
35	Pinsent Masons	22.4%	22.4%
36	RPC	26.0%	30.0%
37	Shakespeare Martineau	17.4%	22.9%
38	Shoosmiths	15.4%	13.0%
39	Simmons & Simmons	26.1%	27.9%
40	Slaughter and May	14.3%	38.5%
41	Stephenson Harwood	24.7%	39.8%
42	Stewarts Law	18.6%	17.7%
43	Taylor Wessing	13.5%	32.8%
44	TLT	20.2%	29.2%
45	Travers Smith	14.7%	39.1%
46	Trowers & Hamlin*	18.1%	13.6%
47	Watson Farley & Williams	22.9%	36.4%
48	Weightmans	17.1%	27.4%
49	Withers	19.4%	32.0%
50	Womble Bond Dickinson	29.3%	37.4%

Source for 2017 ranking by revenue: www.thelawyer.com/top-200-uk-law-firms/.
Source for gender pay gap figures gov.uk – mandatory statistics provided by law firms to gov.uk (https://gender-pay-gap.service.gov.uk/).
* Statistics taken directly from firm's gender pay gap report.
(a) Includes partner earnings – excluding partner earnings, Gateley's (an AIM listed company) mean figure is 18.2% and the median is 32.6%. Because partners are business owners, they are excluded from the regulations and generally the above statistics show the gender pay gap excluding partner earnings.

Table 2. Top 50 law firms in order of revenue – gender pay gap (hourly rate)

No	Firm	Mean gender pay gap %	Median gender pay gap %
1	DLA Piper	17.8%	12.2%
2	Clifford Chance	20.3%	37.2%
3	Allen & Overy	19.8%	27.4%
4	Linklaters	23.2%	39.1%
5	Hogan Lovells	15.3%	26.0%
6	Freshfields Bruckhaus Deringer	13.9%	13.3%
7	Norton Rose Fulbright	17.0%	23.8%
8	Herbert Smith Freehills*	19.0%	38.8%
9	CMS	17.3%	32.8%
10	Ashurst	24.8%	32.7%
11	Clyde & Co	22.4%	38.2%
12	Slaughter and May	14.3%	38.5%
13	Eversheds Sunderland	23.2%	25.4%
14	Pinsent Masons	22.4%	22.4%
15	Gowling WLG*	25.0%	25.0%
16	Simmons & Simmons	26.1%	27.9%
17	Bird & Bird	14.5%	27.6%
18	Berwin Leighton Paisner	22.3%	36.8%
19	Taylor Wessing	13.5%	32.8%
20	Irwin Mitchell	12.8%	15.9%
21	Osborne Clarke	24.4%	31.7%
22	DAC Beachcroft	27.1%	22.6%
23	DWF	23.7%	26.5%
24	Addleshaw Goddard*	23.8%	16.4%
25	Stephenson Harwood	24.7%	39.8%
26	Withers	19.4%	32.0%
27	Macfarlanes	16.5%	37.1%
28	Holman Fenwick Willan	17.4%	30.9%
29	Fieldfisher	16.5%	22.2%
30	Watson Farley & Williams	22.9%	36.4%
31	Mishcon de Reya	17.3%	37.4%
32	Kennedys	22.2%	25.9%
33	Charles Russell Speechlys	22.0%	28.1%
34	Travers Smith	14.7%	39.1%
35	Shoosmiths	15.4%	13.0%
36	BLM	18.4%	22.4%
37	Womble Bond Dickinson	29.3%	37.4%
38	RPC	26.0%	30.0%
39	Hill Dickinson	25.9%	23.5%
40	Trowers & Hamlin*	18.1%	13.6%
41	Weightmans	17.1%	27.4%
42	Mills & Reeve	20.1%	34.2%

No	Firm	Mean gender pay gap %	Median gender pay gap %
43	Ince & Co	28.0%	42.0%
44	Burges Salmon	23.3%	35.2%
45	Stewarts Law	18.6%	17.7%
46	Gateley (a)	47.7%	51.6%
47	TLT	20.2%	29.2%
48	Blake Morgan	26.1%	32.8%
49	Freeths*	11.0%	8.8%
50	Shakespeare Martineau	17.4%	22.9%

Source for 2017 ranking by revenue: www.thelawyer.com/top-200-uk-law-firms/.
Source for gender pay gap figures gov.uk – mandatory statistics provided by law firms to gov.uk (https://gender-pay-gap.service.gov.uk/).
* Statistics taken directly from firm's gender pay gap report.
(a) Includes partner earnings – excluding partner earnings, Gateley's (an AIM listed company) mean figure is 18.2% and the median is 32.6%. Because partners are business owners, they are excluded from the regulations and generally the above statistics show the gender pay gap excluding partner earnings.

Table 3. Top 50 law firms ranked by mean gender pay gap (hourly rate)

No	Firm	Mean gender pay gap %	Median gender pay gap %
1	Gateley (a)	47.7%	51.6%
2	Womble Bond Dickinson	29.3%	37.4%
3	Ince & Co	28.0%	42.0%
4	DAC Beachcroft	27.1%	22.6%
5	Blake Morgan	26.1%	32.8%
6	Simmons & Simmons	26.1%	27.9%
7	RPC	26.0%	30.0%
8	Hill Dickinson	25.9%	23.5%
9	Gowling WLG*	25.0%	25.0%
10	Ashurst	24.8%	32.7%
11	Stephenson Harwood	24.7%	39.8%
12	Osborne Clarke	24.4%	31.7%
13	Addleshaw Goddard*	23.8%	16.4%
14	DWF	23.7%	26.5%
15	Burges Salmon	23.3%	35.2%
16	Eversheds Sunderland	23.2%	25.4%
17	Linklaters	23.2%	39.1%
18	Watson Farley & Williams	22.9%	36.4%
19	Clyde & Co	22.4%	38.2%
20	Pinsent Masons	22.4%	22.4%
21	Berwin Leighton Paisner	22.3%	36.8%

22	Kennedys	22.2%	25.9%
23	Charles Russell Speechlys	22.0%	28.1%
24	Clifford Chance	20.3%	37.2%
25	TLT	20.2%	29.2%
26	Mills & Reeve	20.1%	34.2%
27	Allen & Overy	19.8%	27.4%
28	Withers	19.4%	32.0%
29	Herbert Smith Freehills*	19.0%	38.8%
30	Stewarts Law	18.6%	17.7%
31	BLM	18.4%	22.4%
32	Trowers & Hamlin*	18.1%	13.6%
33	DLA Piper	17.8%	12.2%
34	Holman Fenwick Willan	17.4%	30.9%
35	Shakespeare Martineau	17.4%	22.9%
36	CMS	17.3%	32.8%
37	Mishcon de Reya	17.3%	37.4%
38	Weightmans	17.1%	27.4%
39	Norton Rose Fulbright	17.0%	23.8%
40	Fieldfisher	16.5%	22.2%
41	Macfarlanes	16.5%	37.1%
42	Shoosmiths	15.4%	13.0%
43	Hogan Lovells	15.3%	26.0%
44	Travers Smith	14.7%	39.1%
45	Bird & Bird	14.5%	27.6%
46	Slaughter and May	14.3%	38.5%
47	Freshfields Bruckhaus Deringer	13.9%	13.3%
48	Taylor Wessing	13.5%	32.8%
49	Irwin Mitchell	12.8%	15.9%
50	Freeths*	11.0%	8.8%

Source for 2017 ranking by revenue: www.thelawyer.com/top-200-uk-law-firms/.
Source for gender pay gap figures gov.uk – mandatory statistics provided by law firms to gov.uk (https://gender-pay-gap.service.gov.uk/)
* Statistics taken directly from firm's gender pay gap report.
(a) Includes partner earnings – excluding partner earnings, Gateley's (an AIM listed company) mean figure is 18.2% and the median is 32.5%. Because partners are business owners, they are excluded from the regulations and generally the above statistics show the gender pay gap excluding partner earnings.

Table 4. Top 50 firms ranked by median pay gap (hourly rate)

No	Firm	Mean gender pay gap %	Median gender pay gap %
1	Gateley (a)	47.7%	51.6%
2	Ince & Co	28.0%	42.0%
3	Stephenson Harwood	24.7%	39.8%
4	Linklaters	23.2%	39.1%
5	Travers Smith	14.7%	39.1%
6	Herbert Smith Freehills*	19.0%	38.8%
7	Slaughter and May	14.3%	38.5%
8	Clyde & Co	22.4%	38.2%
9	Mishcon de Reya	17.3%	37.4%
10	Womble Bond Dickinson	29.3%	37.4%
11	Clifford Chance	20.3%	37.2%
12	Macfarlanes	16.5%	37.1%
13	Berwin Leighton Paisner	22.3%	36.8%
14	Watson Farley & Williams	22.9%	36.4%
15	Burges Salmon	23.3%	35.2%
16	Mills & Reeve	20.1%	34.2%
17	Blake Morgan	26.1%	32.8%
18	CMS	17.3%	32.8%
19	Taylor Wessing	13.5%	32.8%
20	Ashurst	24.8%	32.7%
21	Withers	19.4%	32.0%
22	Osborne Clarke	24.4%	31.7%
23	Holman Fenwick Willan	17.4%	30.9%
24	RPC	26.0%	30.0%
25	TLT	20.2%	29.2%
26	Charles Russell Speechlys	22.0%	28.1%
27	Simmons & Simmons	26.1%	27.9%
28	Bird & Bird	14.5%	27.6%
29	Allen & Overy	19.8%	27.4%
30	Weightmans	17.1%	27.4%
31	DWF	23.7%	26.5%
32	Hogan Lovells	15.3%	26.0%
33	Kennedys	22.2%	25.9%
34	Eversheds Sunderland	23.2%	25.4%
35	Gowling WLG*	25.0%	25.0%
36	Norton Rose Fulbright	17.0%	23.8%
37	Hill Dickinson	25.9%	23.5%
38	Shakespeare Martineau	17.4%	22.9%
39	DAC Beachcroft	27.1%	22.6%
40	BLM	18.4%	22.4%
41	Pinsent Masons	22.4%	22.4%
42	Fieldfisher	16.5%	22.2%
43	Stewarts Law	18.6%	17.7%

44	Addleshaw Goddard*	23.8%	16.4%
45	Irwin Mitchell	12.8%	15.9%
46	Trowers & Hamlin*	18.1%	13.6%
47	Freshfields Bruckhaus Deringer	13.9%	13.3%
48	Shoosmiths	15.4%	13.0%
49	DLA Piper	17.8%	12.2%
50	Freeths*	11.0%	8.8%

Source for 2017 ranking by revenue: www.thelawyer.com/top-200-uk-law-firms/.
Source for gender pay gap figures gov.uk – mandatory statistics provided by law firms to gov.uk (https://gender-pay-gap.service.gov.uk/)
* Statistics taken directly from firm's gender pay gap report.
(a) Includes partner earnings – excluding partner earnings, Gateley's (an AIM listed company) mean figure is 18.2% and the median is 32.5%. Because partners are business owners, they are excluded from the regulations and generally the above statistics show the gender pay gap excluding partner earnings.

"It is appalling that in the 21st century there is still a big difference between the average earnings of men and women. While I am encouraged that over 10,000 employers have published their data, these figures set out in real terms for the first time some of the challenges and the scale of this issue."

Minister for Women and Equalities Penny Mordaunt

Table 5. Law firms' gender pay gap – bonuses (listed in order of 2017 revenue)

No	Firm	Percentage of female bonus recipients	Percentage of male bonus recipients	Mean bonus gap	Median bonus gap
1	DLA Piper	58.8%	53.3%	53.6%	0%
2	Clifford Chance	55.9%	55.1%	53.2%	50.7%
3	Allen & Overy	53.2%	55.5%	42.1%	23%
4	Linklaters	78.4%	75.9%	57.9%	62.1%
5	Hogan Lovells	54.3%	47.3%	47.9%	62.3%
6	Freshfields Bruckhaus Deringer	64.5%	58.9%	41%	33.3%
7	Norton Rose Fulbright	27.2%	36.7%	36%	31.6%
8	Herbert Smith Freehills*	77%	71%	30%	10.4%
9	CMS	90%	90%	26.9%	30.4%
10	Ashurst	34.1%	44.3%	64.4%	60.2%
11	Clyde & Co	35%	35%	66.7%	53.3%
12	Slaughter and May	91.6%	92.2%	33.3%	54.8%
13	Eversheds Sunderland	69.3%	71%	42.8%	31.3%
14	Pinsent Masons	35.8%	33.9%	47.4%	40%
15	Gowling WLG*	67%	63%	64%	49%
16	Simmons & Simmons	25.8%	29.9%	36.8%	58.8%
17	Bird & Bird	40%	42%	33.5%	48.9%
18	Berwin Leighton Paisner	11.5%	30.3%	56.4%	32.5%
19	Taylor Wessing	50.3%	51%	29.3%	53.5%
20	Irwin Mitchell	24.5%	28.6%	18%	20%
21	Osborne Clarke	77.8%	78.1%	33.2%	36.7%
22	DAC Beachcroft	57.3%	54.2%	44.8%	42%
23	DWF	24%	24.2%	23.6%	15.1%
24	Addleshaw Goddard*	54.9%	60.6%	43.2%	33.3%
25	Stephenson Harwood	30.1%	40.1%	48.2%	62.4%
26	Withers	84.1%	83.6%	54%	7.8%
27	Macfarlanes	94%	94%	31.7%	14.8%
28	Holman Fenwick Willan	92.4%	92.5%	41.1%	54.1%
29	Fieldfisher	64.6%	70.7%	23.3%	0%
30	Watson Farley & Williams	94.6%	96.5%	38.2%	11.7%
31	Mishcon de Reya	54.9%	51.9%	41.9%	50.9%
32	Kennedys	34.3%	33.9%	13.9%	0%
33	Charles Russell Speechlys	41%	39%	50.1%	40%
34	Travers Smith	87.2%	86.4%	37.8%	78.4%
35	Shoosmiths	94%	92%	18%	0%
36	BLM	48.7%	55.2%	26.2%	37.4%
37	Womble Bond Dickinson	23%	34%	45.3%	40%
38	RPC	64%	66%	69%	56%
39	Hill Dickinson	36.6%	35.7%	69.3%	53.4%
40	Trowers & Hamlin	91.8%	93.8%	34.6%	19.9%

continued on next page

41	Weightmans	7.7%	11.9%	42.7%	30%
42	Mills & Reeve	94.9%	97.3%	42.6%	4.5%
43	Ince & Co	66.7%	57.3%	54.1%	19.6%
44	Burges Salmon	88%	86%	39.5%	20.3%
45	Stewarts Law	62.9%	84.3%	26.7%	50%
46	Gateley (a)	64.6%	62.1%	64.7%	43.9%
47	TLT	7.9%	12.6%	64.1%	50%
48	Blake Morgan	44.6%	37.7%	29.6%	25%
49	Freeths*	83.33%	75.21%	38.18%	21.43%
50	Shakespeare Martineau	95%	93%	40.1%	0%

Source for 2017 ranking by revenue: www.thelawyer.com/top-200-uk-law-firms/.
Source for gender pay gap figures gov.uk – mandatory statistics provided by law firms to gov.uk (https://gender-pay-gap.service.gov.uk/)
* Statistics taken directly from firm's gender pay gap report.
(a) Includes partners' bonuses; excluding partners, the mean figure 18.2% and the median is -32.4%.
Because partners are business owners, they are excluded from the regulations and generally the above statistics show the gender pay gap excluding partner earnings.

Table 6. Magic Circle firms' gender pay gap

Firm	Mean gender pay gap including partners	Median gender pay gap including partners	Mean gender pay gap excluding partners	Median gender pay gap excluding partners	Bonus gap mean including partners	Bonus gap median including partners	Percentage of male bonus recipients	Percentage of female bonus recipients
Allen & Overy	61.2(a)	39(a)	19.8(b)	27.4(b)	45.3(a)	28(a)	74.8(a)	79.6(a)
Clifford Chance	66.3(c)	43.6(c)	20.3(b)	37.2(b)	53.2(c, d)	50.7(c, d)	55.1(c)	55.9(c)
Freshfields Bruckhaus Deringer	60.4(c)	34.1(c)	13.9(b)	13.3(b)	42.2(c)	34.2(c)	51.4(c)	62.7(c)
Linklaters	60.3(c)	44.2(c)	23.2(b)	39.1(b)	76.6(c)	73.9(c)	79.2(c)	79.1(c)
Slaughter and May	61.8(c)	41.6(c)	14.3(b)	38.5(b)	33.3(c, d)	54.8(c, d)	78.5(c)	88.6(c)

(a) Source: Allen & Overy UK Pay Gap Report 2018
(b) Source: gov.uk
(c) Source: BEIS Committee
(d) Partners do not receive bonuses

Table 7. US and international law firms' gender pay gap

Firm	Pay gap mean	Pay gap median	Bonus mean	Bonus median	Percentage of male bonus recipients	Percentage of female bonus recipients
White & Case	24.0%	31.0%	45.0%	71.0%	46.0%	44.0%
Reed Smith	14.8%	37.1%	27.1%	13.2%	71.9%	76.9%
Baker McKenzie	17.4%	32.0%	40.3%	29.3%	84.7%	77.4%
Kirkland & Ellis	33.2%	68.2%	62.3%	74.3%	77.4%	77.9%
Dentons	22.4%	34.3%	52.3%	50.7%	61.8%	63.1%
Weil Gotshal & Manges	38.1%	53.3%	50.0%	55.8%	85.0%	86.0%
Mayer Brown	15.3%	34.2%	23.1%	24.1%	38.0%	30.0%
Squire Patton Boggs	27.1%	20.2%	73.8%	50.0%	29.8%	29.7%
Latham & Watkins	39.1%	38.9%	52.3%	83.0%	58.0%	62.0%
Dechert	34.8%	51.0%	67.7%	72.3%	55.8%	65.4%
Shearman & Sterling	39.0%	54.0%	78.0%	55.0%	31.2%	59.0%
Jones Day	32.6%	4.8%	n/a	n/a	n/a	n/a

Source: © Legal Week, https://images.legalweek.com/contrib/content/uploads/documents/378/Gender-Pay-Gap-table-2018_v2.pdf.
Because partners are business owners, they are excluded from the regulations and generally the above statistics show the gender pay gap excluding partner earnings. earnings. They are the mandatory statistics provided to gov.uk.

2. Inadequacies

Many commentators have pointed to flaws in the gender pay data provided. Lewis Silkin highlights a few of the inadequacies:

There can be errors in the collection of the raw data. Usually it involves combining data from multiples sources – data from payroll systems must be combined with gender data from HR systems and often share scheme information that might not be stored in any easily accessible form.

The gender pay gaps that are published are not necessarily an indication of how 'good' an employer is. It is hard to compare one organisation against another (one might outsource their support staff, taking them outside the scope of the regulations; another may not). Also, there are many workplaces which are very predominantly male (eg, manufacturing) that have reported very low gaps (remember, it is about comparing the average woman against the average man – if a company hires no/few men in manufacturing jobs and just a few women in office roles like HR or finance, they can end up with a very 'good' looking gap, but that isn't a reflection on what the workplace is like for a woman there).

Gender pay gap narratives

Law firms provided supporting statements to their gender pay gap statistics. By way of an encouraging example, Withers (which has a female CEO, Margaret Robertson) pointed out in its gender pay gap statement[11] that 40% of its partners are women; and over the past three years the percentage of new female partner promotions has stood at 57% in 2016, 62.5% in 2017 and 62.5% in 2018. The average (mean) partner hourly pay rate is -4.2% and the bonus gaps is -3.1% – both unusually in favour of women. As at most law firms, its secretarial team is 95% female and accounts for 18% of its workforce.

In its supporting statement (and nearly all law firms' supporting statements made similar points), Herbert Smith Freehills said: "[A] large proportion of women in our firm – 22% – work in secretarial roles. If we exclude secretarial roles from our data analysis, our mean pay gap reduces to 8.8% and the median to 13.6%."[12]

Similarly, Farrer & Co says in its supporting statement: "Our analysis found that our current gender pay gap is largely the result of the gender profile of certain roles within the firm, as observed by the gender imbalance in our lower and lower-middle quartiles. The majority of these roles are secretarial, 98.6% of our secretaries being female, and all of our secretaries are in the lower and lower-middle pay quartiles. If we calculate the gender pay gap without including our secretaries' data, the mean pay gap is 6%."[13]

Jonathan Bond, director of HR and learning at Pinsent Masons, told the author:

> In our organisation, the reason why we have a gender pay gap is because it's a structural issue: half our lawyers are female, but 99.6% of our legal PAs are female. We don't want to recruit only women into that role, but only women apply for those roles; and as you might expect, the market rate for a legal PA is much lower than that for an experienced lawyer. Our gender pay gap among our lawyer population is negligible, but it is because the gender pay gap requires you to put every role into just one pot and calculate the average salary. That's the real reason why we have the gender pay gap.

At Pinsent Masons, he continues: "There is a suggestion that men are drawn to the disciplines that pay slightly more – like financial services and mergers and acquisitions – and we have more women in departments like employment, where the market rate is marginally less. The drivers for the market rate are the very unsocial and unpredictable hours that people in banking and mergers and acquisitions have to do. It is pretty negligible, but we are talking about 1% or 2%."

He adds: "I think many law firms have a gap because they are measuring apples against pears – they are measuring PAs and ancillary staff against lawyers."

In fact, nearly every law firm points to occupational segregation of a largely female secretarial force skewing their figures; perhaps more firms should consider career progression for legal secretaries?

1. Treatment of partners' pay

One of the most controversial issues is the treatment of partner pay in the gender pay gap reports. For example, Gateley's gender pay gap is different from that of other top 50 UK law firms. In 2015 Gateley was the first UK law firm to float on the Alternative Investment Market of the London Stock Exchange. As a result, it is a public limited company and no longer has equity partners. All of its partners are employees and therefore their remuneration is included in in its gender pay gap report. Most other law firms have excluded partner earnings from their gender pay gap figures. Partners are outside the scope of the regulations on the grounds that they are seen as business owners rather than employees. The fact that some law firms chose to exclude partner earnings has massively skewed their figures.

As the recent BEIS Committee report on gender pay gap reporting[14] states:

> [O]ne issue that need to be clarified before next year is the way in which the remuneration of equity partners is included in the gender pay figures. The guidance published alongside the Regulations did not require the pay of equity partners in limited liability partnerships (LLPs) to be included in the calculations, as they are not employees and receive a share of the profits made, potentially based in part on length of tenure as a partner. However, as partners receive the highest pay in these companies, their exclusion gives a totally misleading impression of the size of the pay gap. For example, the mean pay gap figure for PwC was 12% without the inclusion of partners, and 33% with them included.

Initially, most of the major legal firms took a different view from the Big Four audit companies and opted not to publish figures including partners. The BEIS report says: "The HR Director at Slaughter and May, Louise Meikle, tried to justify this to the Committee by saying that because they published diversity statistics, the data would not reveal anything new and that they required clearer guidance from the

"Our analysis found that our current gender pay gap is largely the result of the gender profile of certain roles within the firm, as observed by the gender imbalance in our lower and lower-middle quartiles. The majority of these roles are secretarial, 98.6% of our secretaries being female, and all of our secretaries are in the lower and lower-middle pay quartiles. If we calculate the gender pay gap without including our secretaries' data, the mean pay gap is 6%."

Farrer & Co

Government about how to calculate the figures... Their median gender pay gap, including partners, turned out to be 41.6% in 2017. We subsequently wrote to the six 'Magic Circle' law firms asking for their gender pay gap figures, including partners' remuneration."

The BEIS report states that "the gaps for median pay, excluding partners, ranged from 13% to 39%; with partners, the figures were in every case significantly higher, although different methods of calculation inhibit accurate comparison".

The report continues:

> These figures reveal very publicly just how male-dominated the upper echelons of all our most prestigious legal firms currently are. Whilst at junior associate and associate levels, the proportion of women is, respectively, just under and just over 50%, at the level of partner, this figure drops to between 20–24%.... Whilst they pay lip service to their commitment to improving the representation of women, and some have introduced measures aimed at doing so, progress remains painfully slow. For example, in pursuit of a time-unlimited target of 30% women partners, Clifford Chance has seen an increase from 16.5% to only 21% since 2009... It is clear for legal firms, including those claiming that gender diversity had been a strategic priority for many years, it will take many years at the present rate of progress before they begin to look anything like gender-balanced at the senior, rather than more junior levels. We urge them to examine carefully the reasons why the rate of promotion of women to partner level remains generally slow and to redouble efforts to speed things up.

The report concludes: "The exclusion of the highest paid people in organisations makes a nonsense of efforts to understand the scale of, and reasons behind, the gender pay gap. The Government was wrong to omit the remuneration of partners from the figures required in the Regulations."

The BEIS Committee has recommended that the government clarify how data on partner pay should be calculated and include guidance in time for the publication of data next year.

Responding to the BEIS Committee's recommendations on gender pay gap reporting, Law Society of England and Wales Vice President Simon Davis said:[15] "The Law Society supports the inclusion of partner pay alongside employee pay data in gender pay gap reporting to give solicitor firms a useful benchmark and enable an evidence-based action plan to tackle inequalities."

He added: "We are working with the profession to develop a common set of standards that will provide the level of transparency expected by firms' clients, people and the public. Because partner pay is structured differently from salaries, a new reporting method will be required to ensure data is meaningful and helpful for addressing inequalities in pay. We will work with government and other professional and business services to develop an approach that is comparable across firms and industries."

2. The view from the coalface

Jonathan Bond, director of HR and learning at Pinsent Masons, comments:

> *The gender pay gap regulations specified that equity partners should be excluded. It was very clear and specific about that. So we observed that rule. Then we discovered that there was a lot of opinion – public opinion and governmental opinion – that partners should be included even though the government had passed legislation that they shouldn't be, so we undertook a voluntary exercise to run the data with partners included because we want to be transparent. We want to follow the rules. We want to share the information. We want to understand what the picture is in our organisation, so our opinion is that they should be included, but that we didn't do it first time around because the legislation is very specific that they shouldn't be.*

In an email to the author, Michael Burd, chair and partner at Lewis Silkin LLP, pointed to:

> *a practical issue in including equity partners, since the gender pay gap statistics are based on a 'snapshot' of pay on a particular date. But equity partners' pay is generally not paid like salary is. Rather, a monthly 'draw' is paid against anticipated annual profit share, and then 'true up' payments are made later (sometimes over a period of years) after the actual profit figure is known. Obviously, you can then look back and work out what the annual pay of the equity partner was, but that does not fit neatly into the gender pay gap regulations regime. Also, to what extent are those subsequent 'true up' payments to be treated as normal 'pay' or 'bonus'? And to what year should they relate?*
>
> *All of that said, if you want to get a fairer picture of pay differentials, then it makes sense for equity partner pay to be included in some way or other.*

Laura King, partner and global head of HR and talent at Clifford Chance, also commented to the author:

"The introduction of the gender pay gap regulation is really important in terms of opening up a discussion and shining a light on what's going on and making employers think about their practices and making the media aware of the scale of the problem; but we don't think it is the whole solution. We think it is only a tiny part of it. It is about exposing the problem rather than solving it."

Trades Union Congress Women's Officer Scarlet Harris

Currently, the legislation doesn't mandate inclusion of partners, as they are not employees. This is understandable, given the different nature of compensation of partners and their separate equity contribution to a partnership structure. However, as the underlying objective of the legislation is to better understand, and improve, the representation of different genders across the organisation, we believe that this requires a broader analysis which should include our partners. We opted to report figures which included all UK employees and all UK partners based upon total annual compensation, as we considered that this would add to the overall holistic picture and support transparency, debate and change.

3. The union view – what employers should be doing

The Trades Union Congress (TUC), as might be expected, takes a robust approach to the issue. For it, gender pay gap reporting is just the first step towards a more equal society. Scarlet Harris, TUC women's officer, told the author: "The introduction of the gender pay gap regulation is really important in terms of opening up a discussion and shining a light on what's going on and making employers think about their practices and making the media aware of the scale of the problem; but we don't think it is the whole solution. We think it is only a tiny part of it. It is about exposing the problem rather than solving it."

She says there are lots of things employers should be doing:

It might be a straightforward case of pay discrimination where, in a law firm, you have two solicitors effectively doing the same job and the male solicitor is being paid more.

Occupational segregation is another part of it. It is about better-paid sectors being male dominated and the top jobs within these sectors being male dominated; that is very much the case in law, and that is what I think is driving some of the gaps within the big law laws. The other side of the coin are caring responsibilities, work-life balance, women's roles outside of work, women working part time and having career breaks for periods of maternity and then coming back at a lower level. So some of these issues revolve around family leave and caring responsibilities, and how unequally these are shared out in society.

Although it is a wider social problem, there are things employers can do to facilitate women not slipping down the career ladder once they have children – whether it is about having better maternity leave policies, having more flexible working or job shares at a senior level. It is really important to shine a light on the problem, but it is not enough for employers to publish the data. They need to publish a narrative which is explains what is driving the gap in their firm and action plan to say what they are going to do about it. In a law firm, I would be amazed if in most cases it wasn't about occupational segregation, having the majority of partners as men earning significantly more than junior solicitors.

If you are in a profession where there is a culture of very long hours and a culture of networking outside office hours – whether it be journalists having long lunches or lawyers meeting at different clubs – you might find yourself excluded if you are not able to partake, and if you have caring responsibilities you may need to work regular hours. Law firms need to think progressively about workplace policies and about what does not actually need to be done, what core hours need to look like, how much needs to be done late in the evening, how much could be done at home and how much could be done as a job share.

4. The view from the Law Society

The largest international survey of women in the law was completed by the Law Society of England and Wales to mark International Women's Day 2018 in March 2018. Commenting on the results, Law Society Vice President Christina Blacklaws noted:[16]

While more and more women are becoming lawyers, this shift is not yet reflected at more senior levels in the profession.

Unconscious bias in the legal profession is the most commonly identified barrier to career progression for women, while flexible working is seen as a remedy by an overwhelming 91% of respondents to our survey.

Interestingly, while half of all respondents said they thought there had been progress on gender equality over the last five years, there was a significant difference in perception by gender, with 74% of men reporting progress in gender equality compared to only 48% of women.

The findings from the survey included the following:[17]

- 7,781 people responded to the Law Society's Women in the Law survey (5,758 women, 554 men and 1,469 unknown or other).
- 74% of men and 48% of women reported progress on gender equality in the last five years (overall 50%).
- The main perceived barriers to career progression are as follows:
  - unconscious bias (52%) – however, only 11% said that unconscious bias training is consistently carried out in their organisation;

- unacceptable work-life balance demanded to reach senior levels (49%);
- male-oriented traditional networks/routes to promotion (46%); and
- current resistance to flexible working practices (41%).
- 91% of respondents said that flexible working is critical to improving diversity – 52% work in an organisation where flexible working is in place.
- 60% are aware of gender pay gap in their place of work, but only 16% see visible steps being taken to address the gender pay gap.

Achieving
100%
pay parity

1. Barriers to parity

The barriers to pay parity can be consolidated into a few general areas. Law firm Lewis Silkin says: "Women often suffer a 'parenthood penalty' due to childbirth. They can be held back (whether consciously or not by their managers) as a result of taking time out of the business, while not enough men are similarly taking time out. Women will often work part time for childcare reasons, so earning less and also being held back from reaching more senior roles."

The firm's solution is that "men and women need to take equal responsibility – and time away from work – for childcare". Perhaps the current shared parental leave regime is not enough: "[I]s a separate (and equally generous) right to paternity leave needed? There needs to be an expectation that both sexes will have, at some point in their careers, a long period away from work."

Meanwhile, too few men are working in lower-paid positions – for example, as legal secretaries, which are nearly 100% female; and there is all too rarely a ladder from a secretarial role to a lawyer role.

Lewis Silkin's answer to the problem of not enough women in senior positions is to develop a pipeline of female talent, create a mentoring

"Typically, male partner candidates were saying: 'Yes, I'm ready. I'm good enough.' They were being quite bold and quite confident; while females might typically say: 'I need another year or two before I go forward or I need the stepping-stone route' – which is legal director rather than being promoted directly from senior associate to partner. And so women were, on occasion, putting themselves in the slow lane; so we have had to challenge that by saying, 'We think you're good enough.'"

Jonathan Bond, director of HR and learning, Pinsent Masons

scheme to match senior leaders with up-and-comers and invest in training these people in the leadership skills they need.

There are other issues in recruitment: too few women are applying for top jobs and fewer still are shortlisted for new roles, and there are insufficient women on interview panels. Some solutions include broadening recruitment campaigns so that ads are published in areas more likely to be seen by women, requiring recruitment consultants to pass on CVs for women and requiring recruitment panels to feature at least one man and one woman.

There are also solutions to discriminatory pay, bonus and promotion issues. Asking for disclosure of pay can 'lock in' discriminatory pay from previous employers. Bonus criteria can be easier for men to hit than women. Women may be less likely to ask for pay rises compared to men. One solution is not to ask applicants what they were paid in their previous job. Why not simply have a budget for the role and set the pay at that level? It is also important to review bonus criteria regularly.

Another important factor is unconscious bias in decision making for pay, bonus, promotion and work allocation. Perhaps unconscious bias training is the solution?

2. Closing the gap

Jonathan Bond, director of HR and learning at Pinsent Masons, says:

We identified one common thing. Typically, male partner candidates were saying: "Yes, I'm ready. I'm good enough." They were being quite bold and quite confident; while females might typically say: "I need another year or two before I go forward or I need the stepping-stone route" – which is legal director rather than being promoted directly from senior associate to partner. And so women were, on occasion, putting themselves in the slow lane; so we have had to challenge that by saying, "We think you're good enough."

We also have a reciprocal mentoring scheme; the beauty of that is up-and-coming women have benefited from the experience of older men, while older men have seen the organisation through the lens of a younger's man's completely different experience of the firm, which has opened their eyes about this. There has been some unhelpful behaviour or areas identified where I can help. Things like women going on maternity leave and coming back – just being a bit more understanding and supportive of those things, and making sure more people have a mentor. We have a performance integration programme when they come back, so we can get them up to speed. All these things have helped to eliminate the barriers that we have previously had.

Diversity really concerns the client. Diversity comes up frequently. Five years ago, tender documents wouldn't mention diversity. Now it is very common for a tender document to ask for diversity statistics: "We want examples of things you have done to improve diversity in your organisation." It is a great driver. Obviously, if your clients are saying it is important, then it helps partners to appreciate how important diversity is.

It is not just about what you do in your organisation. It is about society. It is about how people are educated. It is about young people's expectations. It is about eliminating unconscious bias in our firm. Law firms are getting a lot better, but there is a lot of work to be done to get to where we want to be.

Michael Burd, chair and partner at Lewis Silkin LLP, told the author:

It does concern me that there is a gender pay gap; I feel we haven't really got a proper handle on the reasons why. I would like to believe it is not inevitable; but clearly, the fact that women shoulder the bulk of childcare responsibilities is a significant factor. Even more significant is the fact that business has not been great at enabling women who return from maternity leave to continue climbing up the career (and pay) ladder.

As you know, I (together with all other commentators I've read) am clear that the gender pay gap figures do not tell you whether there is equal pay among the sexes for equal jobs. That is a different issue. In my experience, the question of whether there is equal pay or not varies significantly from employer to employer.

I asked Burd: "Is it just a historical anomaly because of the fact that people with lots of experience tend to be men, reflecting the composition of the entry of the profession going back a couple of decades?"

He replied:

That may be part of it, though we have gone for some time with large numbers of women entering the profession. I suspect the reasons are much more tied to issues around childcare and maternity return, exacerbated by the fact that we are a service industry operating increasingly in the 24/7 service culture, and the simple fact is that is just not very family friendly. Working out ways to address that is a big challenge.

I don't think there's any one 'fix'. We probably need a whole range of steps to be taken by employers to counter (at least some of) the causes. But ultimately, the only thing that will really shift it is societal change; and that is always frustratingly slow to come about.

Melanie Stancliffe, employment partner at Irwin Mitchell LLP, told the author:

There are more women qualifying into the legal profession than men and two wages are now needed to pay mortgages, so the tide is definitely turning away from old stereotypical perceptions of gender roles. With the Modern Families and other campaigns, we are seeing government intervention to encourage more fathers to take family leave, to remove the perception that it will be the mother taking a break from work. They could do more, such as increasing the rate of pay for co-parents taking family leave from the low flat rates to a percentage of actual pay, as for the start of maternity leave.

Men and women performing the same role should be paid the same pay. It sounds so simple, but that's been the law since 1970 and yet we're still not there. We need to look at the biases in hiring (eg, blind recruitment), in pay reviews and bonus awards (eg, via a third internal person monitoring increases to ensure that they are objective based and not based on any protected characteristic), in promotions (diverse panels choosing against objective competency and performance criteria), in retention after maternity leave (eg, via greater flexibility on return to work) and the equal 'sponsorship' of men and women in an organisation.

All businesses, unless they have no gender pay gap at all, need to be concerned about this issue. Stancliffe warns:

Potential hires are reviewing the pay gap reporting and the narratives to decide which business they want to work for. Some existing employees are speaking with their feet and leaving businesses whose values do not match the reality of the pay and treatment of women in the business. This is not just an external issue about reputation management. This is having a direct impact on the recruitment and retention of talent. Every employer wants to be an employer of choice and some are doing it, championing diversity or raising the wages for co-parents (male or female) to encourage the take-up of shared parental leave. I'm very proud to work with some of these businesses.

The statistics show a range of pay gaps in businesses and in law firms, so one can't simplify. In law firms, the lower-paid roles tend to be held by women and women are more likely to work part time, both of which add to the pay gap; but times they are a-changing.

Good practice in law firms

1. The view from a regional firm

One law firm that already has good practice is Mills & Reeve. Its 2017 gender pay gap report[18] provides two case studies which show how firms can encourage their female employees.

Joanna Davies, principal associate, writes:

> I found a maternity mentor incredibly valuable in navigating the path from preparing to take maternity leave to keeping in touch while off work and finally managing my return on a new part-time working pattern. A maternity mentor offers practical advice and support for dealing with the transition at work. That might include help considering different options for childcare and part-time working arrangements, sharing ideas for maintaining client relationships, and managing a smooth handover with your team.

> For me personally, the most valuable element was the career coaching offered by my mentor. Returning from maternity leave can be a good time to assess your career aspirations and being able to discuss this openly with a mentor, who was another working mum, was invaluable. Having a mentor gives you the benefit of someone else's experience, who has faced the same challenges of balancing a career and children.

"I found a maternity mentor incredibly valuable in navigating the path from preparing to take maternity leave to keeping in touch while off work and finally managing my return on a new part-time working pattern. A maternity mentor offers practical advice and support for dealing with the transition at work. That might include help considering different options for childcare and part-time working arrangements, sharing ideas for maintaining client relationships, and managing a smooth handover with your team."

Joanna Davies, principal associate, Mills & Reeve

There is no easy solution, but Mills & Reeve is open to individuals finding an arrangement that works for them. The maternity mentoring programme signals how Mills & Reeve is committed to supporting women returning to work and progressing their careers. Coming back can be daunting, and having the right support in place helps to show you're truly valued by the firm. After the positive experience I had, I have now become a maternity mentor myself. I'd like to encourage others to use the mentoring as a launch pad to establish, or resume, a fulfilling career.

Jo Grandfield, a Mills & Reeve partner, has had a similar experience at the firm:

Juggling a family and a demanding career involves inevitable compromises. Mills & Reeve has given me the flexibility to work around the needs of my children and still progress my career in the way I wanted and at the pace I needed. I joined Mills & Reeve in 2008 and had my first child the following year. After taking a little under a year's maternity leave, I returned part time. It was difficult to juggle part-time hours as a litigator at that time, as the technology available to assist with flexible working was far less advanced than it is now, and I found striking the right balance a real challenge.

"New technology and different ways of working are the norm at Mills & Reeve. Flexible working is embedded within our culture and supported. We utilise technology to make things work both for us and our clients. There's a culture of 'getting the job done, smartly and efficiently'. What I like most about Mills & Reeve is that flexible working is not considered to be a 'benefit' or 'treat', or something out of the ordinary. It is what we do when we need to do it in a way that ensures it works for everyone – by which I mean both us and the client."

Jo Grandfield, partner, Mills & Reeve

I had my second child in 2012 and took a slightly extended maternity leave before coming back to cover a professional support lawyer's own maternity leave, which enabled me to work fewer hours when my children were very small while keeping up to date with developments in the law.

In 2014, I was given the opportunity to be part of the firm's new team of family lawyers in the capital and so my family and I relocated from Leeds to London. Mills & Reeve did everything it could to support me personally in making the move and to enable the demands of what quickly became a leadership role to fit in with my other commitments. I was promoted to the partnership in 2017 and continue to work part time and flexibly. New technology and different ways of working are the norm at Mills & Reeve. Flexible working is embedded within our culture and supported. We utilise technology to make things work both for us and our clients. There's a culture of "getting the job done, smartly and efficiently". What I like most about Mills & Reeve is that flexible working is not considered to be a "benefit" or "treat", or something out of the ordinary. It is what we do when we need to do it in a way that ensures it works for everyone – by which I mean both us and the client.

Flexible working can be very helpful to families with children or other caring responsibilities. Withers' gender pay statement points out: "We have always had a flexible working policy, irrespective of gender and of caring responsibilities that an individual may have. We are encouraging agile working and currently have 33% of staff working remotely on a regular basis."

2. The view from a Magic Circle firm

Magic Circle firms face particular problems when it comes to the gender pay gap. At Clifford Chance, while there is room for improvement, the supporting statement to its gender pay gap report[19] points to "use of apprenticeship as a potential route". The firm also says that it is introducing gender pay gap reporting to department leaders at key decision points in the organisation, such as pay and promotion, to "increase our focus on reviewing key leadership roles (such as client relationship leadership) for gender balance".

It adds:

We have already changed the balance of several key committees including our London leadership group. Women now make up 50% of the group. The firm has and continues to invest in training for all colleagues around unconscious bias. Additional enhanced training is being arranged for those in management positions.

We have also started to embed discussions around gender balance at a practice area and business function level. We have been running courses to support the career progression of Associates – both male and female ("Building Personal Profile" and "Planning Your Career Success") – and have included a gender balance component in induction courses for Senior Associates and new partners. Career Development Partners are assigned to every Associate – playing a role as a mentor and guide for our lawyers' career development. The firm's leadership wants to promote greater numbers of women and is working towards a target of 30% female partners.

Laura King, partner and global head of HR and talent at Clifford Chance, told the author:

Some of the current gap can be explained by historical promotion rates of women into the partnership. The more senior levels of law firm partnerships represent promotions which took place more than a decade previously. As long as gender-balanced promotion in law firms in the UK continues to improve (which by and large it has over the last decade), it is reasonable to anticipate a slow improvement in the gender pay gap at senior levels. However, it is anticipated that this will require continued momentum, encouragement and monitoring (particularly in relation to those firms with highly differentiated (rather than lockstep seniority-based) partner pay structures). However, partnership gender balance is not the only factor driving gender pay gap within law firms: to a greater mathematical extent, it is driven by the concentration of women in secretarial and administrative roles within the firms. This also bears examination: is it consistent with the market and job seekers that these roles are generally filled by women, or are we not structuring recruitment for these opportunities in the right way for the reality of the market?

3. The view from a top 20 firm

Most firms in their gender pay gap reports make some effort to show how they are responding to the gender pay gap. For example, Gowling WLG[20] says:

We are confident we do not have an equal pay issue. However, we are continuing to take steps to ensure that everyone within the firm has the same career opportunities, allowing them to access salary and bonus progression as they develop and advance through the firm:

- *In 2016, the firm committed to gender targets of 30% women in the partnership by 2026. We have introduced a number of initiatives including unconscious bias training, maternity coaching and mentoring to help us reach that goal, as well as adopting agile working practices for everyone to recognise and support our diverse population.*

- *Our More Women network is driving the practices we need to achieve gender equality at the top of our firm. It provides internal and external networking events, and has helped shape our directors' mentoring programme.*
- *Our Family Matters network supports working parents and anyone with caring responsibilities. It helps them achieve quality of life at home and at work.*
- *Each strand of our diversity programme has a dedicated board sponsor and our board collectively reviews our diversity performance and strategy on a half yearly basis.*
- *Through social mobility, we aim to fill our teams with the best and brightest people from all walks of life. We run a programme supporting those from deprived backgrounds, offering work placements, mentoring and bursaries. Our award-winning Legal Social Mobility Programme gives students work experience in our firm and our clients' organisations.*

Like many other law firms, because of its structural shape and demographics, Gowling WLG admits that it will be challenging to reduce its gender pay gap reported under the regulations dramatically in the foreseeable future. This is not encouraging for young women seeking a career in the law.

Tackling the gender pay gap – government recommendations

The BEIS report has abundant suggestions for tackling the gender pay gap. Indeed, the new transparency and accompanying public scrutiny will, in itself, help to tackle the unacceptably wide gender pay gaps in so many organisations.

The report states:

> Evidence suggests that the reputational damage wrought by the publication of these figures is likely to be the most effective spur to action, and that businesses are under no illusions about this. The introduction of gender pay gap reporting has consequently already had an impact on changing behaviour in many organisations. Several companies have re-examined the statistics they initially published because of the public reaction. But the initial flurry of attention associated with the revelation of the size of the organisations' gaps is likely to fade in a year or two.

However, the BEIS Committee does not believe that "this public naming and shaming on an annual basis will be enough, by itself, to remedy the situation in the long term".

1. Understanding the causes

According to the BEIS Committee, evidence suggests that in general,

"The disclosure of huge differences in the levels of pay between male and female senior executives and those working for the BBC was a catalyst for that organisation to address the unfairness inherent in its own practices. Without this transparency – which the BBC resisted – there would have been no change. Increased transparency may be uncomfortable for some individuals, and needs to be handled with care for data protection reasons, but a cultural shift towards greater transparency on pay is a necessary part of long term efforts to remove the gender pay gap and should be encouraged."

BEIS Committee report

women start on an equal footing, but then do not progress up the promotion ladder as fast or as often as male counterparts, and are less likely to be promoted than men after starting a family.

There is also a maternity penalty and a part-time penalty. The BEIS report further refers to behavioural issues: "Some research indicates that men are far more likely to apply for promotion without the full range of skills required... Laura Hinton from PwC told the committee that that their work had established that women there were as ambitious as men but it took them longer to achieve promotion... They may not be encouraged to push for promotion when they have young children or are reluctant to do so."

Sheila Flavell, chief operating officer of FDM Group, told the committee: "Women lack confidence, and that is a fact ... the main problem we have with returners is that they are not confident; they do not feel they are good enough ... With women, you have to push them. You have to push them and you have to pull them. You have to continuously instil confidence in them, in my experience."

The report cautions: "Businesses and organisations need to be conscious of these factors, particularly when determining support provided for returners and promotion policies."

It continues:

> Other evidence suggests that women are less aggressive than men in negotiating their pay – there may be other factors that tend to be more important to women, such as flexible working – and that they are more resistant to moving, so potentially less inclined to walk away in pay negotiations ...
>
> The disclosure of huge differences in the levels of pay between male and female senior executives and those working for the BBC was a catalyst for that organisation to address the unfairness inherent in its own practices. Without this transparency – which the BBC resisted – there would have been no change. Increased transparency may be uncomfortable for some individuals, and needs to be handled with care for data protection reasons, but a cultural shift towards greater transparency on pay is a necessary part of long term efforts to remove the gender pay gap and should be encouraged.

2. Policies and practices

According to the BEIS Committee: "There are 1,377 employers (13% of the total) with reported gender pay gaps in excess of 30%.... There is undoubtedly a long way to go for many, but success is achievable. For example, Unilever has pursued a swathe of policies which has resulted in half of all management positions being taken by women and a pay gap of 2% in favour of women."

There is a case for simplicity, as well as transparency: the founder of the Equal Pay Portal, Sheila Wild, told the committee: "As a rule of thumb, the simpler the pay system, the less likely you are to get a gender pay gap."

The BEIS report identifies a range of initiatives, practices and policies that have been used to address the gender pay gap, which include the following:

- encouraging flexible working throughout the organisation, including at senior levels;
- providing the same paternity leave as maternity leave;
- providing training on unconscious bias and addressing assumptions around women's preferences in allocating work, which can lead to management deliberately not allocating high-profile work involving unsocial hours to women with children;
- introducing enhanced benefits for family leave and parental leave policies, including specific programmes for those returning;
- establishing women's networks and informal discussion groups;
- improving outreach work and promoting engagement by encouraging companies in traditionally male sectors to use 'female-friendly branding' with universities and local schools, to address cultural perceptions;
- initiating targeted and comprehensive recruitment campaigns, including careful use of language, aimed at recruiting more female science, technology, engineering and mathematics, technology and computer science school leavers, apprentices and graduates;
- using gender-neutral application forms and shortlists;
- focusing support on promoting women into lower tiers of management early, as well as developing the pipeline of talent in more senior management roles;
- supporting women through the provision of individual mentoring, coaching and sponsorship, to help them navigate the career ladder;
- reverse mentoring, to enable senior executives to better understand the career experiences of junior women in the organisation;
- championing women in industry, through networking activities and sponsored awards events;
- reviewing mechanisms for allocating work, to check that they are not subject to biased assumptions;

- setting targets for recruiting women or for achieving a gender balance in specific parts of the business, including at senior levels;
- addressing complex pay systems, including strong elements of discretionary pay – such as bonuses – which are vulnerable to conscious and unconscious bias, and policies on allowances and incentives that increase the pay gap; and
- undertaking equal pay audits, to examine the extent and causes of gender pay gaps and check that equal pay is being provided for work of equal value. Are pay rates between different functions warranted? For example, should traditionally 'male' roles in more physical roles be paid more highly than more 'female' roles in administrative support and human resources? Are any such gaps justified and to what extent do these contribute to the pay gap?

3. Setting targets

One way to achieve higher representation of women at a senior level is to set targets. The BEIS report says that organisations should be ambitious and set stretching targets that are right for their circumstances:

"Witnesses argued that it may in fact be unrealistic to pursue a pay gap of exactly zero due to the effects of routine changes in personnel, but a range of plus or minus 3% would be indicative of a properly gender balanced workforce that companies could be expected to maintain. We agree. A step by step by step approach with tiered targets over time may be a sensible way forward."

BEIS Committee report

Companies with a high gender pay gap may reasonably expect the reduction and eradication of their pay gap to take longer. For example, Linklaters set itself a target of doubling the number of women on its governance and management boards, albeit to a still-low 30%... Witnesses argued that it may in fact be unrealistic to pursue a pay gap of exactly zero due to the effects of routine changes in personnel, but a range of plus or minus 3% would be indicative of a properly gender balanced workforce that companies could be expected to maintain. We agree. A step by step by step approach with tiered targets over time may be a sensible way forward.

In setting targets, organisations should balance the pressure for securing visible signs of progress in the short term with the need to secure long term sustainable solutions. For example, if a company, in an effort to make long-term improvements in the pipeline of senior women, recruits a higher proportion of women at the start of their career, their pay gap may actually increase for a few years, before these women rise through the ranks. This underlines the need for a narrative to accompany the bald figures.

4. "What Works" guidance

The Government Equalities Office has also published new "What Works" guidance[21] for companies to help them improve the recruitment and progression of women and close their gender pay gap. The guidance was produced in partnership with the Behavioural Insights Team.

The guidance, including full details of the research evidence, has been published on the gender pay gap website at https://gender-pay-gap.service.gov.uk/.

The Government Equalities Office guidance recommends the following actions to help close the gender pay gap, which "have been tested in real world settings and found to have a positive impact":[22]

- *Include multiple women in shortlists for recruitment and promotions:* "When putting together a shortlist of qualified candidates, make sure more than one woman is included. Shortlists with only one woman do not increase the chance of a woman being selected."
- *Use skills-based assessment tasks in recruitment:* "Rather than relying only on interviews, ask candidates to perform tasks they would be expected to perform in the role they are applying for. Use their performance on those tasks to assess their suitability for the role. Standardise the tasks and how they are scored to ensure fairness across candidates."
- *Use structured interviews for recruitment and promotions:*

"Structured and unstructured interviews both have strengths and weaknesses, but unstructured interviews are more likely to allow unfair bias to creep in and influence decisions according to What Works guidance."

- "Ask exactly the same questions of all candidates in a predetermined order and format."
- "Grade the responses using pre-specified, standardised criteria. This makes the responses comparable and reduces the impact of unconscious bias."

- *Encourage salary negotiation by showing salary ranges:* "Women are less likely to negotiate their pay. This is partly because women are put off if they are not sure about what a reasonable offer is. Employers should clearly communicate the salary range on offer for a role to encourage women to negotiate their salary. This helps the applicant know what they can reasonably expect... If the salary for a role is negotiable, employers should state this clearly as this can also encourage women to negotiate. If women negotiate their salaries more, they will end up with salaries that more closely match the salaries of men."

- *Introduce transparency to promotion, pay and reward processes:* "Transparency means being open about processes, policies and criteria for decision-making. This means employees are clear what is involved, and that managers understand that their decisions need to be objective and evidence-based because those decisions can be reviewed by others. Introducing transparency to promotion, pay and reward processes can reduce pay inequalities."

- *Appoint diversity managers and/or diversity taskforces:* "Diversity managers and task forces monitor talent management processes (such as recruitment or promotions) and diversity within the organisation. They can reduce biased decisions in recruitment and promotion because people who make decisions know that their decision may be reviewed. This accountability can improve the representation of women in your organisation. Diversity managers should:
  - Have a senior/executive role within the organisation
  - Have visibility of internal data
  - Be in the position to ask for more information on why decisions were made
  - Be empowered to develop and implement diversity strategies and policies."

Conclusion: Has the gender pay gap exercise been worthwhile?

1. Views on the ground

It is too early to say whether mandatory reporting has had or will have any impact on recruitment and winning clients.

In an interview with the author, Jonathan Bond, director of HR and learning at Pinsent Masons, said: "It is a worthwhile exercise collecting this data. There will be a lot of organisations that haven't ever thought about this issue and that may be paying men and women differently for no good reason."

Gender pay gap reporting does take up a lot of time, as Bond explains:

> I have got an analyst in the HR team who has recorded the time. He has spent 270 hours on this, so I think collectively we have spent over 1,000 hours on this exercise.

> We have an analyst, an employment lawyer advising. I have a project manager. I am involved. A senior partner is involved and I hold press briefings and coordinate with other law firms. We have done a whole road show on this. I did a webinar for 420 people internal within the organisation. That's an hour, but about three hours to prepare for and one hour follow-up; so it goes on and on.

To do it properly, you have to spend large amounts of time and be very careful with the detail, check and verify it; and we are already doing this exercise for next year, so it does take a lot of time.

For some organisations that haven't looked at the issue before, it has a shone a spotlight on pay differentials. For us, it did not tell us anything we didn't already know; but all the same, we welcome the opportunity to play our part to do it in the right way.

Some people are equating equal pay with gender pay and thinking that if you have a gender pay gap, you are obviously paying women and men differently for the same work – which is the wrong conclusion, because equal pay differentials have been illegal for 40 years; but of course, people don't always appreciate that. For all those reasons, it does take a lot of time; but mostly it has moved the dialogue forward and been a really good thing.

Michael Burd, chair and partner, at Lewis Silkin, told the author: "I definitely believe that it is right that society should want to understand the extent and reasons for the gender pay gap, and to take sensible steps to reduce it. I am not convinced that the way in which the regulations require the statistics to be collated is most effective to that end, but it is nevertheless worthwhile – and collecting more meaningful statistics would be even more worthwhile. And yes, it is time consuming."

Laura King, partner and global head of HR and talent at Clifford Chance, told the author that collecting gender pay gap statistics "did take time and resource – data had to be collected, verified, audited and discussed. However, this was a worthwhile exercise: it is valuable to look at the organisation from the perspective of gender pay and to foster discussion as to why a gap may exist in particular areas or functions. We also analysed the data to understand where we had issues and why. The discussion took place at all levels, reinvigorated our focus and stimulated further change".

Melanie Stancliffe, employment partner at Irwin Mitchell, agreed:

Producing the gender pay gap reporting information is time consuming. However, it is necessary – firstly, to comply with the legal obligation on businesses with 250 or more employees to publish their data; and secondarily, as an annual snapshot of how the business is rewarding its staff. It requires businesses to hold up a mirror to what can be unconscious or previously unknown pay disparities between people performing similar roles and allows the business to use that information in its pay review decisions to address the inequalities.

We live in 2018. It should worry anyone that there is a need for pay gaps to be analysed and published; there should be equal pay without the need for scrutiny and publication. In the absence of that equality, it is a necessary tool to force employers to look at their pay, retention, flexible working, sponsorship and other practices.

2. Time for effective action

The light that mandatory reporting has shone on the gender pay gap has caused a media sensation, but will it have a lasting effect? As almost every company has been shamed, has it just desensitised us to the issues?

An internal note prepared by Lewis Silkin recognises this problem:[23]

Many of the gender pay gap reports that are available say similar things: "We know we don't have an equal pay problem"; "Our gap is not as bad as those of our competitors"; 'There's not enough women in this area"; "We're doing some initiatives that we hope will have an impact in the long term, but we won't be able to tell for ages whether they actually do."

So, given this, is it easy to be cynical about the effect of the regulations.

"We live in 2018. It should worry anyone that there is a need for pay gaps to be analysed and published; there should be equal pay without the need for scrutiny and publication. In the absence of that equality, it is a necessary tool to force employers to look at their pay, retention, flexible working, sponsorship and other practices."

Melanie Stancliffe, employment partner at Irwin Mitchell

But actually, it's woken many organisations up. It's caused them to start thinking about issues in a way that previously they might not. It has galvanised them into action.

Our experience has been that many clients have been thinking about how these issues play out in their workplaces and what they can do to solve them. For example, we've been asked to help develop mentoring and women in leadership schemes, equal pay audits and reviews of recruitment procedures.

Clifford Chance's King acknowledges that in Magic Circle firms, culture is clearly a factor to be examined: "Recruitment, attrition, development, promotion and role models all play a role. While historical promotion rates have not traditionally assisted, the (albeit slowly) growing percentage of female partners at large international firms is helping to redress the balance. The legislation and reporting provide an important framework for firms to benchmark their progress."

Thus far, there is little concrete evidence that mandatory reporting has had a significant impact on recruitment and winning clients, apart from anecdotal evidence; but it is highly likely that people (especially women) will be increasingly reluctant to want to work for employers that have high pay gaps. The oxygen of publicity will make sure that this issue remains at the top of the HR agenda for many years to come.

But the last word must be given to the influential BEIS report: "Organisations cannot rely on excuses about societal attitudes and trends to avoid examining their own contribution, conscious or otherwise, to their gender pay gaps and the effectiveness of their measures to address them. They must take responsibility for closing these gaps by taking effective action."

Appendix I. Gender pay gap reporting: overview

Advisory, Conciliation and Arbitration Service and Government Equalities Office

Employers with 250 or more employees must publish and report specific figures about their gender pay gap

Mandatory gender pay gap reporting

From 2017, any organisation that has 250 or more employees must publish and report specific figures about their gender pay gap.

The gender pay gap is the difference between the average earnings of men and women, expressed relative to men's earnings. For example, 'women earn 15% less than men per hour'.

Employers must both:

- publish their gender pay gap data and a written statement on their public-facing website
- report their data to government online – using the gender pay gap reporting service.

If your organisation has fewer than 250 employees, it can publish and report voluntarily but is not obliged to do so.

When you must publish and report

The figures must be calculated using a specific reference date – this is called the 'snapshot date'. The snapshot date each year is:

- 31 March for public sector organisations
- 5 April for businesses and charities

Organisations must publish within a year of the snapshot date. For example, businesses and charities must publish by 4 April each year. Public sector organisations must publish by 30 March each year.

'Relevant employer'

Your organisation will be a 'relevant employer' and must publish and report if it has 250 or more employees who are based in England, Scotland or Wales.

The legal entity that is the 'relevant employer' (for example, the private limited company or public sector organisation) must register with and report to the Gender pay gap reporting service.

If your organisation is a 'relevant employer' and runs multiple payrolls (for example payrolls for different departments or business functions), you must merge relevant data from all your payrolls and report one set of figures for your organisation.

Private sector group structures

Private sector organisations that are part of a group must report individually if they are 'relevant employers'.

Additionally, corporate groups can voluntarily report combined figures for the entire group.

Public sector organisations – who must report and publish

Public sector organisations include government departments, the armed forces, local authorities, NHS bodies and most schools.

If your organisation is listed in Schedule 2 to the Equality Act 2010 (Specific Duties and Public Authorities) Regulations 2017, you must publish and report your gender pay gap data following the public sector rules (using a snapshot date of 31 March). Your HR department should be able to tell you if this applies to you.

If you're a public sector employer and not listed in Schedule 19 to the

Equality Act 2010, you must publish and report – but follow the private and voluntary sector regulations. You must use a snapshot date of 5 April.

Government departments must publish and report gender pay gap data covering all of their employees – including their executive agencies (as these are the same legal entity). Executive agencies can also voluntarily report for their own organisations.

Arms-length bodies (such as statutory non-departmental bodies) must publish and report as they are separate legal entities from their sponsor department.

If you're a school of any kind and your legal entity employs 250 or more people, you must report and publish. You won't be included in your local education authority's gender pay gap reporting.

For maintained schools in and out of federations, the governing body is responsible for publishing their own gender pay gap reports. Maintained schools may be foundation, community, voluntary, nursery or special schools.

For academies in and out of chains, and for free schools, the proprietor is responsible for reporting their gender pay gap data. Independent and private schools should follow the private sector gender pay reporting regulations (using 5 April as the snapshot date). The legal employer must report and publish their gender pay gap data.

If your organisation is a Scottish or Welsh public authority and you already follow gender pay gap reporting requirements in your country, you don't need to publish or report under these rules.

Who counts as an 'employee'

The definition of 'employee' for gender pay gap reporting includes:

- people who have a contract of employment with your organisation
- workers and agency workers (those with a contract to do work or provide services)
- some self-employed people (where they must personally perform the work)

When to count agency workers and self-employed people in your organisation

If your organisation uses agency workers or service companies, they count as part of the headcount of the agency or service company that provides them – not your organisation.

You must include self-employed people in your organisation's calculations if they must personally perform work for you and you have the data available, for example where a project initiation document exists or a schedule of fees is in place.

Part-time workers and job-sharing

You must count each part-time worker as one employee for gender pay gap reporting purposes.

If you use job-share arrangements, every employee within a job-share counts as one employee. So, if 2 people job-share, they count as 2 employees for gender pay gap reporting purposes.

When employees have more than one job with your organisation, you can either choose to count them according to how many employment contracts they have or as one employee. Your organisation can choose the most appropriate approach – but it will help the accuracy of your figures if you consistently apply what you decide.

Overseas workers and international jobs

As a general rule, you must count an employee based overseas if they have an employment contract subject to English, Scottish or Welsh law.

Partners in partnerships

You don't have to include partners in traditional partnerships and limited liability partnerships in your calculations. This is because partners take a share of the organisation's profits, which is not directly comparable with employees' pay.

Data you must publish and report

You must publish on your organisation's public-facing website and report to government your organisation's:

- mean gender pay gap in hourly pay
- median gender pay gap in hourly pay
- mean bonus gender pay gap
- median bonus gender pay gap
- proportion of males and females receiving a bonus payment
- proportion of males and females in each pay quartile

You'll need to:

- gather specific information from your payroll
- use this information to make your calculations
- publish a written statement on your organisation's website which confirms the accuracy of your calculations

You must publish and report your organisation's figures if you're a 'relevant employer'. The Equality and Human Rights Commission can enforce any failure to comply with the regulations.

Support to manage and improve your organisation's gender pay gap
You can read about the actions employers can take to close the gender pay gap.

You can also get advice on managing your organisation's gender pay gap from the Advisory, Conciliation and Arbitration Service (Acas) website.

Acas offers:

- practical guidance on identifying gender pay issues and improving them
- training courses and events on calculating your organisation's gender pay gap
- tools and support to communicate with your employees about gender pay issues

Appendix II. Gender pay gap reporting: make your calculations

Advisory, Conciliation and Arbitration Service and Government Equalities Office

Gender pay gap figures you'll need to calculate

You must publish and report your organisation's:

- mean gender pay gap in hourly pay
- median gender pay gap in hourly pay
- mean bonus gender pay gap
- median bonus gender pay gap
- proportion of males and females receiving a bonus payment
- proportion of males and females in each pay quartile

You can report your figures to government as either whole percentages or percentages rounded to one decimal place.

To make the calculations, you must have gathered specific data from your organisation's payroll. This data is based on figures drawn from a specific date each year – called the 'snapshot date'.

- 5 April is the snapshot date for businesses and charities.
- 31 March is the snapshot date for public sector organisations.

Hourly pay figures you must calculate

You must calculate your organisation's gender pay gap in hourly pay, as both a:

- mean figure (the difference between the average of men's and women's pay)
- median figure (the difference between the midpoints in the ranges of men's and women's pay)

Mean gender pay gap in hourly pay: how to calculate

1. Add together the hourly pay rates of all male full-pay relevant employees

2. Divide this figure by the number of male full-pay employees – this gives you the mean hourly pay rate for men

3. Add together the hourly pay rates of all female full-pay relevant employees

4. Divide this figure by the number of female full-pay employees – this gives you the mean hourly pay rate for women

5. Subtract the mean hourly pay rate for women from the mean hourly pay rate for men

6. Divide the result by the mean hourly pay rate for men

7. Multiply the result by 100 – this gives you the mean gender pay gap in hourly pay as a percentage of men's pay

Median gender pay gap in hourly pay: how to calculate

1. Arrange the hourly pay rates of all male full-pay relevant employees from highest to lowest

2. Find the hourly pay rate that is in the middle of the range – this gives you the median hourly rate of pay for men

3. Arrange the hourly pay rates of all female full-pay relevant employees from highest to lowest

4. Find the hourly pay rate that is in the middle of the range – this gives you the median hourly rate of pay for women

5. Subtract the median hourly pay rate for women from the median hourly pay rate for men

6. Divide the result by the median hourly pay rate for men

7. Multiply the result by 100 – this gives you the median gender pay gap in hourly pay as a percentage of mens' pay

Bonus pay figures you must calculate
You must calculate your organisation's figures for the:

*   proportion of males and females who got bonus payments
*   mean gender pay gap in bonus payments
*   median gender pay gap in bonus payment

Proportion of males and females who got bonus payments: how to calculate

1. Get the number of male relevant employees who were paid bonus pay in the 12 months to the snapshot date

2. Divide this by the number of male relevant employees

3. Multiply the result by 100 – this gives you the percentage of males who were paid a bonus

4. Get the number of female relevant employees who were paid bonus pay in the 12 months to the snapshot date

5. Divide this by the number of female relevant employees

6. Multiply the result by 100 – this gives you the percentage of females who were paid a bonus

Mean gender pay gap in bonus pay: how to calculate

1. Add together the bonus payments made to all male relevant employees in the 12 months to the snapshot date

2. Divide this figure by the number of male relevant employees – this gives you the mean amount of bonus pay for men

3. Add together the bonus payments made to all female relevant employees in the 12 months to the snapshot date

4. Divide this figure by the number of female relevant employees – this gives you the mean amount of bonus pay for women

5. Subtract the mean bonus amount for women from the mean bonus amount for men

6. Divide the result by the mean bonus amount for men

7. Multiply the result by 100 – this gives you the mean gender pay gap for bonuses as a percentage of men's pay

Median gender pay gap in bonus pay: how to calculate

1. Arrange the bonus pay amounts paid to all male relevant employees in the year to the snapshot date from highest to lowest

2. Find the bonus pay amount that is in the middle of the range – this gives you the median bonus pay figure for men

3. Arrange the bonus pay amounts paid to all female relevant employees in the year to the snapshot date from highest to lowest

4. Find the bonus pay amount that is in the middle of the range – this gives you the median bonus pay figure for women

5. Subtract the median bonus pay figure for women from the median bonus pay figure for men

6. Divide the result by the median bonus pay figure for men

7. Multiply the result by 100 – this gives you the median gender pay gap for bonus pay as a percentage of men's pay

Gender pay gap quartile figures you must calculate

You must calculate your organisation's figures to show the proportion of male and female full-pay relevant employees in four pay bands.

To do this, you need to:

- rank your full-pay relevant employees from highest to lowest paid
- divide this into 4 equal parts ('quartiles')
- work out the percentage of men and women in each of the 4 parts

Gender pay gap quartile figures: how to calculate

1. Divide into quartiles

Get a listing of the hourly pay rate of all your organisation's full-pay relevant employees in the pay period that covers the snapshot date.

Divide this list into 4 quartiles, with an equal number of employees in each section. From highest paid to lowest paid, these quartiles will be the:

- upper quartile
- upper middle quartile
- lower middle quartile
- lower quartile

If the number of employees isn't divisible by 4, distribute them as evenly as possible. For example, if you have 322 full-pay relevant employees an equal split would mean 80 employees in each quartile, with 2 employees left over.

To distribute the numbers as evenly as possible, you can add one employee to the lower quartile and one employee to the upper middle quartile.

This means there are 81 employees in the lower quartile, 80 employees in the lower middle quartile, 81 employees in the upper middle quartile, and 80 employees in the upper quartile.

2. Check the gender distribution of matching hourly rates

If there are employees on the same hourly rate of pay crossing between quartiles, make sure that males and females are split as evenly as possible across the quartiles.

For example, you have 322 full-pay relevant employees and have split the list into quartiles. 40 staff all have the same hourly rate of pay – 36 are female and 4 are male. Of them, 10 have fallen into the lower quartile, while 30 have fallen into the lower middle quartile.

To evenly distribute these staff by gender, you can see that for every 9 females listed, one male should be listed with them. You should list 9 female employees and one male employee in the lower quartile, and 27 female employees and 3 male employees in the lower middle quartile.

3. Work out the percentage of males and females in each quartile

For each quartile, you need to:

- divide the number of male full-pay relevant employees by the total number of full-pay relevant employees and multiply by 100 – this gives you the percentage of males in the quartile
- divide the number of female full-pay relevant employees by the total number of full-pay relevant employees and multiply by 100 – this gives you the percentage of females in the quartile

Notes

1 www.parliament.uk/business/committees/committees-a-z/commons-select/business-energy-industrial-strategy/news-parliament-2017/gender-pay-gap-report-published-17-19/.

2 https://first100years.org.uk/about-us/.

3 https://first100years.org.uk/carrie-morrison-interview/.

4 www.lawsociety.org.uk/news/press-releases/historic-shift-as-women-outnumber-men-practising-as-solicitors/.

5 www.lawsociety.org.uk/support-services/research-trends/annual-statistics-report-2017/.

6 www.sra.org.uk/solicitors/diversity-toolkit/diverse-law-firms.page.

7 www.legislation.gov.uk/uksi/2017/172/pdfs/uksi_20170172_en.pdf.

8 Lewis Silkin internal note.

9 www.gov.uk/guidance/gender-pay-gap-who-needs-to-report.

10 www.gov.uk/government/news/100-of-uk-employers-publish-gender-pay-gap-data.

11 https://marketing.withersworldwide.com/reaction/emsdocuments/PDFs/29722_GenderPayGapStatement_HR_revised.pdf.

12 www.herbertsmithfreehills.com/sites/contenthub_mothership/files/Herbert%20Smith%20Freehills%20gender%20pay%20gap%20report.pdf.

13 www.farrer.co.uk/globalassets/policies/gender-pay-gap-reporting-2017.pdf.

14 https://publications.parliament.uk/pa/cm201719/cmselect/cmbeis/928/92802.htm.

15 www.lawsociety.org.uk/news/press-releases/developing-common-gender-pay-gap-reporting-standards/.

16 www.lawsociety.org.uk/news/press-releases/largest-ever-survey-on-gender-equality-in-legal-profession/.

17 www.lawsociety.org.uk/news/press-releases/largest-ever-survey-on-gender-equality-in-legal-profession/.

18 www.mills-reeve.com/files/Uploads/Documents/PDF/mills-reeve-gender-pay-gap-report-2017.pdf.

19 www.cliffordchance.com/content/dam/cliffordchance/About_us/Gender-Pay-Gap-Report-2017.pdf.

20 https://gowlingwlg.com/en/gender-pay-gap-report.

21 https://gender-pay-gap.service.gov.uk/actions-to-close-the-gap/effective-actions.

22 https://gender-pay-gap.service.gov.uk/actions-to-close-the-gap/effective-actions.

23 Lewis Silkin internal note.

Acknowledgements

This special report would not have been possible without the help and advice of many experts, including numerous trade union officials, employment lawyers and HR professionals. Special thanks are due to the following individuals and firms for all their time and expertise: Jonathan Bond, director of HR and learning, Pinsent Masons; Harriet Beaumont, press officer, The Law Society; Michael Burd, chair and partner, Lewis Silkin LLP; Penny Cogher, partner, Irwin Mitchell LLP; Scarlet Harris, Trades Union Congress women's officer; Laura King, partner, global head of HR and talent, Clifford Chance LLP; and Melanie Stancliffe, employment partner, Irwin Mitchell LLP. Their valuable insight has added so much context to the report.

I would also like to thank the following law firms for allowing me to quote from their gender pay gap reports, whose narrative was particularly illuminating: Clifford Chance, Farrer & Co, Gowling WLG and Mills & Reeve.

The author is also particularly grateful to Rachel Reeves MP, chair of the BEIS Committee, whose seminal report on gender pay reporting greatly inspired much of the content of this research.

The research from the Government Equalities Office on closing the gender pay gap was also invaluable.

Finally, I would like to thank the publisher, Sian O'Neill, managing director of Globe Law and Business, for her perspicacity in suggesting to the author such a topical and important subject for research.

Stephanie Hawthorne
September 2018

About the author

Stephanie Hawthorne
Freelance journalist and editor
sjhawthorne@btopenworld.com

Stephanie Hawthorne has been a full-time freelance journalist since April 2017, after editing *Pensions World* magazine for 28 years. Her other editorships included *Counsel* (the journal of the Bar of England and Wales) and its offspring, *Money Matters*, from 1997 to November 2007; and *Charity World*. An honours law graduate of King's College London and winner of numerous prizes for financial journalism, Ms Hawthorne started her financial career in 1980 as a researcher/marketing specialist for a national independent financial adviser and subsequently a leading life office, and then moved on to *Insurance Age, Planned Savings* and *Financial Times' Money Management*.

An occasional broadcaster on BBC, Sky and Channel 5, as well as on radio, she has contributed articles to the *Financial Times*, the *Mail on Sunday*, *The Times*, *The Sunday Times*, *The Sunday Telegraph* and *The Observer*, as well as numerous magazines on property, personal finance, the law and human resources.